Butterflies of the World

Discover, Learn & Explore Butterflies from Around the World

Rose Brown

Published by The Crackajack Company
Imprint: Brainy Bubs
ISBN: 978-81-69067-57-7

Text and concept by Rose Brown
This book is intended for educational and entertainment purposes only.
First Edition, 2026

Monarch Butterfly

USA, Mexico

Did you know?

Monarchs migrate thousands of miles every year!

Blue Morpho

Brazil

Did you know? Its wings look blue but are actually transparent!

Swallowtail Butterfly

India

Did you know? Swallowtails have tail-like extensions on their wings!

Glasswing Butterfly

Central America

Did you know? Its wings are see-through like glass!

Painted Lady

Worldwide

Did you know? Painted ladies are found on almost every continent!

Peacock Butterfly

Europe

Did you know? Its wings have eye spots to scare predators!

Red Admiral

North America, Europe

Did you know? Red admirals are fast flyers and very strong!

Zebra Longwing

Florida, USA

Did you know? It feeds on pollen, not just nectar!

Ulysses Butterfly

Australia

Did you know? It is one of the brightest blue butterflies in the world!

Rajah Brooke's Birdwing

Malaysia

Did you know? It is Malaysia's national butterfly!

Common Jezebel

India

Did you know? Its bright colors warn predators it tastes bad!

Mourning Cloak

Canada

Did you know? It lives longer than most butterflies!

Green Hairstreak

United Kingdom

Did you know? Its wings look like tiny green leaves!

Comma Butterfly

Europe

Did you know? It has a comma-shaped mark on its wings!

Purple Emperor

United Kingdom

Did you know? It prefers tree sap over flowers!

African Giant Swallowtail

Africa

Did you know? It is one of Africa's largest butterflies!

Scarlet Mormon

Asia

Did you know? Females mimic other butterflies to stay safe!

Atlas Moth

Asia

Did you know? It looks like a butterfly but is actually a moth!

Cairns Birdwing

Australia

Did you know? It is Australia's largest butterfly!

Julia Butterfly

South America

Did you know? It has long, narrow wings for gliding!

Paper Kite Butterfly

Southeast Asia

Did you know? It floats slowly like paper in the wind!

Malachite Butterfly

Central & South America

Did you know? Its wings have bright green patterns that stand out!

Question Mark Butterfly

North America

Did you know? It has a tiny question mark shape on its wings!

Metalmark Butterfly

South America

Did you know? Some have shiny, metallic-looking wings!

Tailed Jay Butterfly

India, Southeast Asia

Did you know? It is a fast flier and hard to catch!

Curious for more?
Explore the Did You Know? series by Brainy Bubs, an imprint of The Crackajack Company.
From animals and nature to food and fun facts-there's always something new to discover.

Featuring titles like Dogs of the World, Cats of the World, and Dinosaurs of the World-each with a companion storybook and coloring book.

Enjoyed this? We'd love your review.

9 788169 067577

Printed at Repro India Ltd.